HONEYCOMB

1

St Macarius
P R E S S

First edition © 2023 St Macarius Press

Monastery of Saint Macarius the Great
P.O. Box 2780
Cairo—Egypt

E-mail: info@stmacariuspress.com
Website: www. stmacariuspress.com
Telegram channel: t.me/stmacariuspress
Facebook page: www.facebook.com/stmacariuspress

MATTHEW THE POOR

CHRIST ALONE
SUFFICES

EDITED AND TRANSLATED FROM ARABIC BY

*MONKS FROM
THE MONASTERY OF SAINT MACARIUS*

ST MACARIUS PRESS

MONASTERY OF SAINT MACARIUS THE GREAT (EGYPT)

Original Title
Ḥāǧatunā Ilā al-Masīḥ

ISBN
978-1-7350713-6-7

Series
Honeycomb

Edition and Translation from Arabic
Monks from the Monastery of Saint Macarius

Cover Painting
"Christ Leads the Soul to the Light"
by Ladislav Záborský

Cover
David Georgy

Format
5" x 8"

Pages
23

INTRODUCTION

In 1975, during the Great Lent, Fr. Matthew the Poor delivered a speech to the monks of the Monastery of St. Macarius on the eve of the Sunday of the Prodigal Son. The main thought of his homily was very simple yet very powerful: Christ is the sole real need of our lives. He intended to say with simple words how the centrality of Christ in our lives is paramount and how all our problems, both personal and interpersonal, are caused by the lack of His divine presence. When Christ appears in our lives, miracles happen, as He is capable of reconciling human weaknesses with spiritual realities, as He possesses in Himself both humanity and divinity and is the mediator between the divine and human realms.

Very often as Christians we only need to wait for Christ's manifestation in our lives as it presents a valuable opportunity for people around us to believe in Him and obtain salvation and eternal life. In fact, the reason people around us are unhappy with our lifestyle as Christians is not Christ Himself, but the lack of His presence in our words and actions. He gives taste to everything we say and do. Yet, only Christ possesses the capacity to manifest Himself, given His unattainable stature as the apex of all that exists in both heaven and earth. Our utmost requirement is to encounter His arrival, accept Him, and subsequently permit Him to communicate and operate through us.

It is time to recenter our existence on Christ Himself, rather than our personal abilities, values, aspirations, egotisms, malevolencies, or desires for superficial worldly recognition, which we may disguise under the guise of Christ. We impede our path to God by prioritizing our egos over our love for Christ. We often tend to conceal the authentic Christ from the world's perception because we perceive ourselves as morally upright and neglect to accept Christ's Cross which is the foundation of His work within us.

We are called today to embody the Pauline verses that states, "For we do not preach ourselves, but Christ Jesus the Lord, and ourselves your bondservants for Jesus' sake" (2 Cor. 4:5). We must divest ourselves of our egocentric tendencies and instead adopt a Christocentric perspective, prioritizing our spiritual selves over our temporal identities.

Yes, we are in dire need for Christ!

***

St. Macarius Press is delighted to inaugurate a new series entitled "Honeycomb." After so many years of perusing and contemplating Fr. Matthew the Poor's writings, we have concluded that the best verse to describe his words is, "Beautiful words are like honeycombs" (Prov. 16:24). This is why the series will provide concise texts to be savored and digested slowly in order to nourish our spiritual life. These jewels will act as spiritual capsules to strengthen our love for Christ and desire to serve Him and our brethren.

DURING MY EARLY CHRISTIAN life, the greatest experience that strongly drew my attention was that whenever I felt a sense of lacking in my relationships—be it with others, the Church, or the monks—I became distressed and agonized to the extent that my energy, ministry, and influence upon people were consequently weakened.

However, the moment I approached the person of my Lord Jesus and felt Him as though He was returning after an absence of whose length I was always the cause, my heart would leap with joy. My mind would regather in one fell swoop so that all sense of want, need, and imperfection fell away from me, allowing Christ to rise over the horizon of my whole life. Then I saw Him more than all my needs and felt His fullness overflowing and sweeping my life in the tide of His love while I surrender to Him in a way that surpasses all understanding.

In the same manner, I had this sense whenever I was greatly troubled with numerous thoughts about the ways of God, His dealings with people, or His care for one person as well as for the many. My spirit was then sorely distressed within me to the point of suffocation. For I was always eager to see God's supremacy at all levels—in mercy, justice, chastening, in tender fatherhood, sovereignty, or retribution—and thus I remained torn asunder by conflicting feelings that gave me neither rest nor peace. But once I felt Christ approaching me, my soul calmed down immediately, all my questions and worries vanished, and Christ appeared transcending all my intellectual scales concerning mercy or justice, fatherhood or sovereignty. At such moments, Christ reveals to me the mystery of His will.

Through these two experiences, I have been assured that Christ is the sole need of our lives.

The more distant we are from Him, the greater our reliance on many things of this world, and the more our worrying develops regarding particulars or generalities in our lives.

Why then does Christ's person seem in this manner as the fullness of everything? There is one answer that suffices for this question and many others also. We must realize that humanity comprises within itself two conflicting worlds: the physical and the spiritual. The sum of these two together may appear as a richness inherent in the human nature, but it comes at an exorbitant price. All the high standards belonging to the realm of the spirit that permeates the human are matched by a material decaying reality which, during life, may reach low and ignoble examples.

For instance, a man may kill his brother for a morsel of bread or sell his heavenly heritage for a stew of lentils (cf. Gen. 25:34). The history of civilization, philosophy, and science demonstrates that there is no hope of establishing a natural reconciliation between the tension and laceration inherent in the human being and between the high standards of the spirit and the reality of the flesh, whether through the intervention of wisdom, the refinement of skills, the simple observance of God's commandments, or even punishment.

As soon as human instincts rage, we rebel against all spiritual values, and a temporary spiritual blindness overpowers and drives us to commit the grossest transgressions, even against ourselves.

Here Christ appears in His full humanity and full divinity as the greatest mystery that reconciled both all the human reality— apparent in passions and instincts, dealings with others, time, needs, infirmities, and failures—with the spiritual ideals, or rather with God Himself. This reconciliation is perfect, perpetual, and eternal, and profoundly rooted in the depths of us, for all that belongs to Christ belongs to us.

Christ is both humanity's and God's mystery. He is our mystery because He has penetrated the depths of God's nature. He is God's mystery because He has penetrated the depths of our nature. To enter the light of this mystery, we must recognize that this reconciliation is not based on a theory—no matter how complex—or the simple fulfilment of commands. The reconciliation accomplished by Christ is a personal reconciliation accomplished in Christ Himself, not by our power but by His power, and the result surpasses human understanding. It is sufficient to realize that when reconciliation was accomplished through the Incarnation and Crucifixion of Christ, it encompassed the entirety of humanity in the person of Jesus, who now represents humanity before the Father.

We are reconciled with ourselves, for God was reconciled with us in the body of our humanity that belongs to Christ, which He took from us. Hence, we say confidently and succinctly that we are reconciled with God in Christ. This highly personal reconciliation was a unique mediation undertaken by this sole

Mediator, Christ, between God and humanity, giving rise to a new force that penetrated not only the world but also heaven.

The lesser and more feeble image of our Christianity is our vain attempt to apply the commandments of Jesus Christ to our daily problems without the Lord Jesus Himself. On the contrary, a sturdy and excellent image is obtained when the person of Christ enters our lives. Then all our problems fall at once, and we rise to the level of Jesus' commandments without the least of personal mastery.

Attempting to accomplish Christ's commandments without Him—which is impossible—leads Christian believers to experience daily bitterness and inner laceration since they are completely incapable of fulfilling the commandments, although they love them. Therefore, Christ laid down the commandment so that we may prove by it His presence. As the Scripture says:

> Test yourselves. Do you not know yourselves, that Jesus Christ is in you?—unless indeed you are

disqualified (2 Cor. 13:5).

Hence the Lord says: "He who has My commandments and keeps them, it is he who loves Me" (John 14:21).

In this sense, the one who loves Him is the one who is able to obey His commandments. In other words, the person of Christ comes first, followed by all that is Christ's.

Christians must always declare their faith in front of non-Christians and Christians alike. This persistent demand places us in a constant state of tension. We are obligated to rise to the level of the truth so that we may perceive and reveal it, as well as to the level of faith so that we may act in accordance with the truth before we declare it, lest we disgrace ourselves and Christ alike.

Yet, who can reveal Christ, since Christ is unattainable in His stature, the pinnacle of all that is in heaven and earth, He who recapitulates everything in His own person? Above all, He is the visible image of God, who is invisible.

Therefore, who can preach or even try to explicate Him? Human mind? Impossible! Eloquence and logic? Impossible!

Christ alone has the ability to reveal Himself. When I feel His presence, I drop all my defenses; or rather they fall off of their own accord, because He alone is the voice of my truth and faith, speaking within me. Even when He does not, He is able to reveal Himself in innumerable ways and with an ineffable mystery, for Christ's person is an infinite power that reveals itself in us without any effort on our part. Rather, our efforts are the major impediment to Christ's revelation. Our greatest need is to experience His presence in us, receive Him with our entire being, and then allow Him to speak and act within us.

People's discontentment with our Christian way of life is because of the absence of Christ in our lives, and not at all because of the person of Christ. If Christ in His divinity were ever living in our lives, no one would find fault with His divinity.

People find an occasion of stumbling in Christ because we place Him on an equal footing with other needs and wants such as our daily bread and even pleasures, entertainments, sciences, and politics. Due to this, Christ appears within us a thousand times smaller than His true stature. Therefore, if Christ is God, then He must be higher and greater than everything in our lives and even greater than our lives themselves.

Our dire need is that our Christian life must be Christ Himself and not our own principles, ambitions, pride, malice, or lust for boasting, honor, and vain worldly glory that we conceal behind the name of Christ.

People do not at all despise Christ. Christ is beloved, and in fact, He is referred to as the "Son of Love" (cf. Col. 1:13). He is in fact *love* with all its depths that everyone desires. People despise our conduct, behavior, and false qualities that we untruthfully and hypocritically show in the name of Christ.

The distinction between Christianity and Christ has become more apparent than ever in our lives, provoking a backlash against us. Our actions, deeds, and words appear to be Christian on the surface, but they do not emanate from Christ, lacking His Spirit and pure aroma. Thus, it is not surprising that people dislike our Christian life.

Our direst need remains to turn once more to the person of Christ so that He may manifest Himself in our lives. Then emerges a genuine revival where our fallacious deeds are swept away, giving place to the true deeds of Christ which will bear witness to Him without any interference by our dead strokes of genius. In fact, people should be led to Christ Himself and not our earthly persons. Do we accept this fact? The major conundrum that obstructs our way to Christ is that we are steadfast to our egos rather than Christ. When we face times of danger or fatigue, it is our egos that appear and not Christ.

The most dangerous aspect of this deception is that we perceive ourselves to be good. Due to this, we see no reason to abandon our egos and embrace Christ. Consequently, the true Christ remains hidden from people's eyes and ears. Even when we sometimes perceive ourselves as wretched, hypocrites, crooked, living a deceptive life because we preach Christ while He is completely absent from our lives, we are incapable of transformation because we lack the conviction to take the risk and die so that Christ may resurrect us for Himself anew.

Life in terms of this world is delectable and comforting to the ego that seeks its own glory. Particularly when the ego takes a Christian mask—thus showing a fabricated glory—that can be unmasked only by those who possess the true light of Christ. When will we believe and live according to the Pauline verse that says, "For we preach Christ Jesus the Lord, and ourselves your servants for Jesus' sake" (2 Cor. 4:5)?

Numerous church preachers present their egos disguised under the teachings of Christ causing people to stumble at Christ. The blame and disgrace were not placed on them but rather on the weakened Christ within them. The one who bears witness to Christ must receive from Christ and give to others in return. This is the essence and significance of testimony, which is enacted through the mediation of the Holy Spirit, who knows everything that belongs to Christ and profoundly longs to fittingly testify to Him in us. How often have we displeased the Holy Spirit and obstructed His witness by using the testimony of Jesus for our own glory and advantage? We desperately need to be delivered from our egos. Are we ready for this?

Who can read the life of Jesus Christ and not feel in the depths of their hearts that He is the most magnificent and clear image of God? If God is like Christ, then God really loves mankind as a tender and infinitely omnipotent Father. As Christ says: "He who has seen Me has seen the Father" (John 14:9).

Humanity will remain miserable until it finds God, and it will not find God except in Christ. Therefore, Christ should find in our lives an opportunity to prove His eternal power and godhead, so that people may believe that He is truly the Son of God, attain salvation and eternal life through Him, and truly see the Father in Him. But we are blamed for impeding belief in Christ since we present our egos instead of the true Christ. Consequently, our humanity is glorified at the expense of His divinity.

The redemptive work of Christ consists in our becoming like Him, bearing His conduct and qualities once He fills our lives and reigns over us, not through teaching and instruction, but rather as St. Paul teaches, "That Christ may dwell in your hearts by faith" (Eph. 3:7).

When Christ lives in us and we consequently adopt His conduct, this indicates that humanity has transcended itself and bypassed all of its impotence, disease, and death, entering a phase of glorification that has nothing to do with its deadly, earthly heritage. This is our new creation, which is coupled with Christ's divine power to elevate us above our egos and cause us to enter through His power and effective life into the realm of the divine action and freedom. Then we will freely, consciously, and joyfully respond to God and all of His inspirations, carefully and restlessly. This is the future of our new creation in Christ, and this is our new birth. Thus, Christ was appropriately called the second Adam.

How then can we be born to God without Christ? This is impossible. Let us never forget that Christ founded His work for humanity upon the Cross. Although the Cross entered Christ's life primarily as a redemptive act, He gave it to us as an example of life and conduct. If we do not live and think according to the principle of the Cross, we will never realize Christ's mightiness which He attained through the Cross, nor will we comprehend and appreciate the true significance of His redemption.

But if we experience and taste the Cross in our lives with consciousness and joy, this will be the mystical entrance to the knowledge of Christ and the experience of the extraordinary greatness of His power toward us. Then, through communion in the sufferings of the Cross, we enter into an eternal covenant with Christ as heirs of all the Father's heavenly glories and consolations.

How marvelous is the mystery of Christ, and how much more so is the mystery of man in Christ!

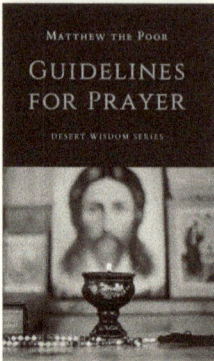

Guidelines for Prayer

MATTHEW THE POOR

If only you knew that the Holy Spirit is the One Who pours love into your heart, imparts to you humility, endows you with peace of heart, strengthens your faith in God and your hope in eternal life, illuminates your insight to recognize the truth and the will of God, and even ignites your heart with the spirit of prayer! It is He who incites you to stand in vigilance with strength and zeal that surpass the ability of the flesh. If only you knew this, then you would realize the great profit that can be reaped from prayer.

FATHER MATTHEW THE POOR (MATTA EL-MASKEEN) (1919–2006) is the refounder and the spiritual father of the Monastery of St. Macarius the Great, Wādī al-Naṭrūn, Egypt. He has greatly contributed to the revival of the Coptic monastic life and has played a significant role in the rediscovery of the early Church Fathers. Father Matthew has been a great advocate of Christian unity. He has hundreds of publications in numerous fields only some of which have been translated so far.

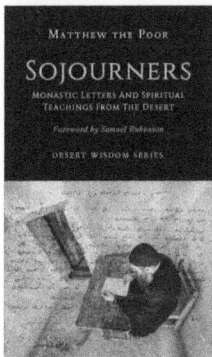

MATTHEW THE POOR
SOJOURNERS
MONASTIC LETTERS AND SPIRITUAL
TEACHINGS FROM THE DESERT
Foreword by Samuel Rubenson
DESERT WISDOM SERIES

Sojourners

MATTHEW THE POOR

The secrets of the journey stipulate certain rules. We should always feel that we are sojourners, pilgrims seeking their eternal homeland. This feeling should not disappear from our heart, mind, or body for a single moment. Fire can be quenched with a little water, but love, if it really burns within one's heart, nothing can quench it;—neither disdain, nor contempt, nor hostility, nor humiliation, nor indifference.

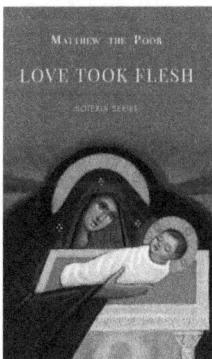

MATTHEW THE POOR
LOVE TOOK FLESH
SOTERIA SERIES

Love Took Flesh

MATTHEW THE POOR

Today, after the sterility of spirit that had befallen our two ancestors, humanity has become fertile. Today has been born to man a Son who is called an everlasting God. Today, we celebrate the birth of the first-fruit of humanity, the first-born among many brethren, the head of the spiritual Church that fills Heaven. Love took flesh; sacrifice became a body.

.

www.ingramcontent.com/pod-product-compliance
Lightning Source LLC
Chambersburg PA
CBHW030013040426
42337CB00012BA/759